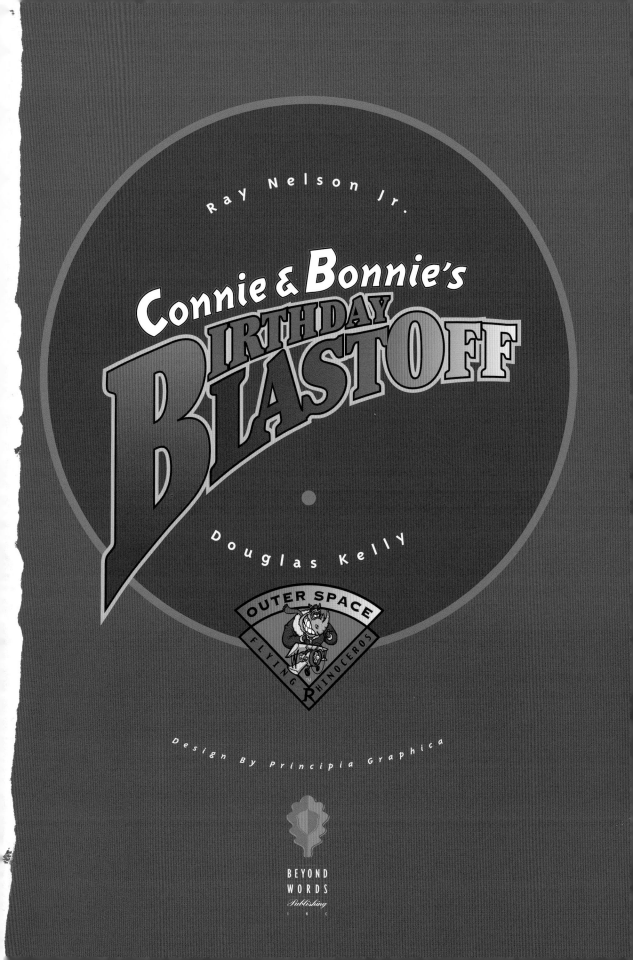

Ray Nelson Jr.

Connie & Bonnie's
BIRTHDAY BLASTOFF

Douglas Kelly

OUTER SPACE

FLYING RHINOCEROS

Design By Principia Graphica

BEYOND
WORDS
Publishing
INC

FOR PAUL AND JOAN CRAIG

Thank you for your friendship and support

ABOUT FLYING RHINOCEROS BOOKS

Flying Rhinoceros books are dedicated to the education and entertainment of elementary school students. *Flying Rhinoceros also offers curriculum/activity packs to accompany all the books.* For more information or to request a catalog, please contact Beyond Words Publishing, Inc.

Beyond Words Publishing, Inc.

4443 NE Airport Road

Hillsboro, Oregon 97124-6074

1-800-284-9673 · 503-693-8700

Library of Congress Catalog Card Number: 95-078726

ISBN: 1-885223-26-9

Produced in the United States of America by SunWest Graphics, Inc., Bridgetown Printing, and Lincoln & Allen Bindery. Printed on recycled paper using soy-based inks.

Distributed to the book trade by Publishers Group West.

OTHER BOOKS FROM FLYING RHINOCEROS:

The Seven Seas of Billy's Bathtub *(Ocean and sea life)*

Greetings from America: Postcards from Donovan Willoughby *(U.S. geography)*

Wooden Teeth and Jelly Beans: The Tupperman Files *(U.S. presidents)*

Shrews Can't Hoop!? *(Self-esteem)*

A Dinosaur Ate My Homework *(Dinosaurs)*

Cartoon Handbook and Field Guide *(How to cartoon)*

INTRODUCTION For as long as anyone can remember, human beings, young and old, have been curious about what is in outer space. The solar system has been a constant source of intrigue and wonderment. It has only been recently that man has actually had the capabilities to travel out beyond the Earth's atmosphere. I was fortunate enough to be one of the early pioneers in space travel.

Bouncing around on the moon with Neil Armstrong on that first lunar landing, July 20, 1969, was great fun. Our stay was too brief, but we left some important experiments and brought back those precious first few pounds of moon rocks that thrilled earthbound scientists. Our traveling companion, Mike Collins, orbited the moon and brought us back home after rendezvous. He said, "Apollo was about leaving" [the Earth]. True, but we were sure glad to return home to our families.

For me to be one of the first group of men to orbit the Earth, walk in space, and then walk on the moon, I had to work extremely hard. I had to study and train to make sure that I was prepared for the challenges that I would face. Through a good education, you too can be prepared for the challenges life has in store for you.

I can't think of any better topic for you to start learning about than outer space.

Enjoy your journey!

Buzz Aldrin

Author's note: Buzz Aldrin is one of 24 men to reach the moon and one of 12 to actually walk on the moon.

The Oregon Museum of Science and Industry is an independent, scientific, educational, and cultural resource center dedicated to improving the public's understanding of science and technology. As a non-profit, non-tax-based organization, OMSI utilizes interactive exhibitry and supportive information to present subjects in the physical, biological, mathematical, life, space, and natural sciences, technology, and industry.

All educational material in "Connie & Bonnie's Birthday Blastoff" has been gathered and verified in cooperation with Jim Todd and his staff at The Oregon Museum of Science and Industry.

OMSI

It was nobody's fault, just a simple mistake, that started with presents and candles and cake.

FOR YOU SEE...

ON THE PLANET OF PLUTO, in deep outer space, a grand birthday party was soon to take place. The event had been planned to the smallest detail — invitations were sent via *Milky Way Mail.*

That's when it happened — the simple mistake. A stray asteroid caused the mailship to quake. Invitations to a party in honor of birth were unharmed — **EXCEPT ONE,** which sailed down to Earth.

INVITATION

At that very same time, out taking a hike, were identical twins who look nothing alike. Connie is tall and always wears red, while Bonnie is short with a great big ol' head.

"We've hiked all about, from mountain to shore — there's no way around it, this place is a bore! We need some adventure: a new stomping ground. A place with excitement, where secrets abound."

Just then and there, sailing down from the sky, an envelope fluttered and caught Connie's eye. "What's this? Take a peek — is it the answer we seek?" "Quit stalling!" yelled Bonnie. "Just read it, you geek!"

BIRTHDAY PARTY

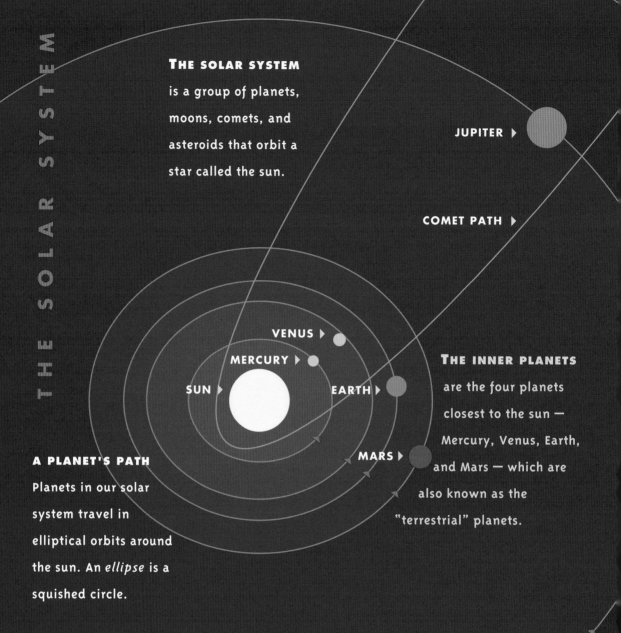

THE SOLAR SYSTEM
is a group of planets, moons, comets, and asteroids that orbit a star called the sun.

JUPITER ▶

COMET PATH ▶

VENUS ▶

MERCURY ▶

SUN ▶

EARTH ▶

THE INNER PLANETS
are the four planets closest to the sun — Mercury, Venus, Earth, and Mars — which are also known as the "terrestrial" planets.

MARS ▶

A PLANET'S PATH
Planets in our solar system travel in elliptical orbits around the sun. An *ellipse* is a squished circle.

"**YAHOO**!" exclaimed Connie, with a smile on her face. "We're invited to party in deep outer space. Tonight is the night — we have no time to waste! We need to get dressed and pick a gift with some taste."

Bonnie stopped cold and scratched her big head— she was now overcome by a feeling of dread. "The party is out in the Final Frontier, which sounds like it's much too far to be near!"

HOW LONG IS A DAY? The time it takes a planet to make one complete rotation (turn) on its axis. A *rotation* is the spinning of a planet on its axis. An *axis* is an imaginary line through the center of a sphere. A planet spins on its axis like a spinning top. It takes 24 hours for Earth to make one rotation. Venus has the longest day. One Venus day equals 243 Earth days. Jupiter has the shortest. One Jupiter day is only 9.8 Earth hours! Most planets in our solar system rotate counter-clockwise. Venus, Pluto, and Uranus are the only ones that rotate clockwise.

AXIS

ROTATION

SATURN ▶

URANUS ▶

REVOLUTION · ORBIT

PARTY
PARTY
PARTY
ON PLUTO ▶ ●

THE OUTER PLANETS are the five planets farthest from the sun — Jupiter, Saturn, Uranus, Neptune, and Pluto.

HOW LONG IS A YEAR? The time it takes a planet to make one complete revolution (trip) around the sun. A *revolution* is one orbit around the sun. All the planets revolve counterclockwise. An *orbit* is the curved path of a planet, satellite, or spacecraft as it goes around another object. One Earth year is 365 days. One Mercury year is only 88 Earth days. One Pluto year equals 248 Earth years!

◀ NEPTUNE

WHEN: Tonight
WHAT: Birthday Party
WHERE: Pluto

"Have no fear," spoke up Connie, "Now stop all the fuss. In science, last year, I got a double A-plus! We just need a spaceship to fly to the sky. We can do it, I know, if we give it a try."

So the identical twins, who look nothing alike, rolled up their sleeves, gave their pants a good hike, then fitted the pieces, with sputters and hissing. The white kitchen sink was the only thing missing.

"We're finished!" they cried, not a moment to spare. The twins hopped in their craft and began to prepare. "Ten!" hollered Connie, "Nine, eight," and then "Seven!" Which was followed by Bonnie quickly adding, "Eleven!"

TEN, NINE, EIGHT, SEVEN, SIX...

Now,

Bonnie
was brave
and her wit
had some bite, but
to be perfectly honest,
she was not really bright.
With the countdown unfinished, the
box started to rise. In a burst of orange
flames they shot through the skies.

The fumes from the smoke caused Bonnie
to cough, "What the heck kind of fuel did
you use to lift off?" Then Connie replied,
"You'll think that it's silly, but all that I
used was Dad's special chili."

ESCAPE VELOCITY is the speed a spacecraft must travel to break away from the

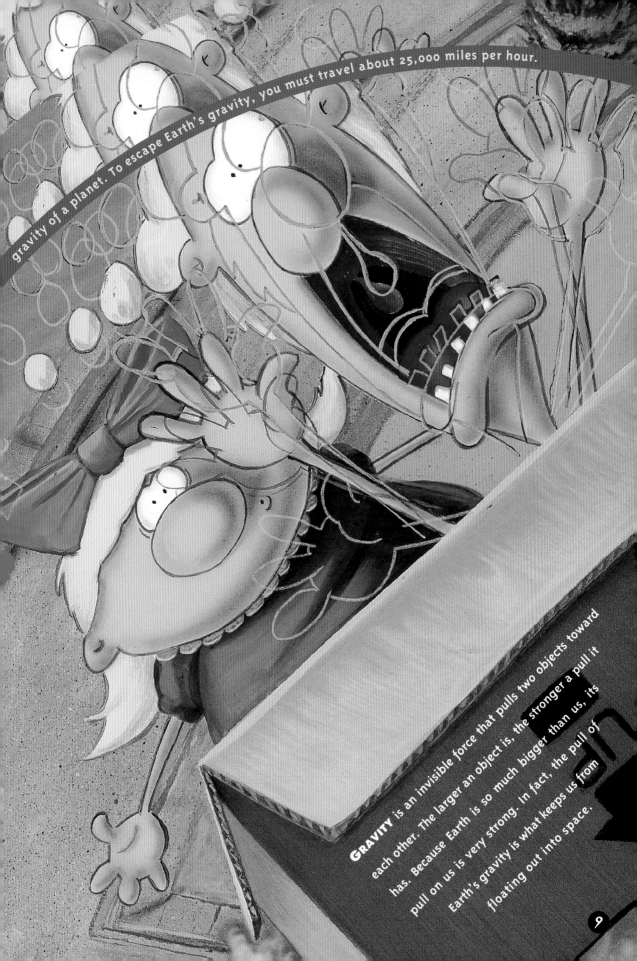

gravity of a planet. To escape Earth's gravity, you must travel about 25,000 miles per hour.

GRAVITY is an invisible force that pulls two objects toward each other. The larger an object is, the stronger a pull it has. Because Earth is so much bigger than us, its pull on us is very strong. In fact, the pull of Earth's gravity is what keeps us from floating out into space.

SPACE SHUTTLE COLUMBIA

APRIL 12, 1981 The first manned spacecraft to orbit the Earth and touch down on a runway.

HUBBLE SPACE TELESCOPE - APRIL 25, 1990 The largest telescope sent into space by NASA. It was dropped off 380 miles above the Earth. Within weeks, it was sending photographs back to Earth of deep-space objects with detail never seen before.

GEMINI 3 - MARCH 23, 1965 Gemini 3 was the first rocket to orbit the Earth with a two-man crew. ▶

SALYUT - APRIL 19, 1971 Soviet cosmonauts lived for record periods of time aboard these space stations.

TELSTAR 1 - JULY 10, 1962 The first communications satellite able to send television pictures across the Atlantic.

APOLLO 7 OCTOBER 11, 1968 The first project to test a craft's ability to travel to the moon.

VOSTOK 1 - APRIL 12, 1961 ▶ Yuri Gagarin was the first man to orbit the Earth. In 1963, Valentina Tereshkova was the first woman in space in Vostok 6.

FRIENDSHIP 7 ▶ FEBRUARY 20, 1962 John Glenn was the first American to orbit the Earth.

EXPLORER 1 JANUARY 31, 1958 The first artificial U.S. satellite to orbit the earth.

SPUTNIK - OCTOBER 4, 1957 The first artificial satellite to orbit the Earth.

ROCKET

POWER

is what a spacecraft uses to blast off into space. A rocket engine burns fuel, forming gases that rush out beneath the rocket, pushing it upward. It's like releasing a full balloon without tying the open end — the air quickly escapes, pushing the balloon away.

MANNED MANEUVERING UNIT, or MMU - 1984

Astronaut Bruce McCandless used the MMU in the first spacewalk to take place without a cord attached to a spacecraft.

"**L**ook!" Bonnie yelled, scared out of her pants, "The people have shrunk — they all look like ants!" Invitation in lap, Connie checked out the map. "If we follow directions, this should be a snap!"

11

(1969) U.S. lunar module ▶

The near side of the moon

The near side of the moon is the side facing Earth. Some people see a face in the moon.

EARTH ▲

ROUGH ROAD AHEAD The moon is covered by many craters. They were formed billions of years ago by meteors slamming into the moon's surface. The craters are many different sizes — some as big as 150 miles across and several miles deep, others only a few inches wide.

NO SWIMMING Early astronomers thought the smooth areas on the moon's surface were seas of water. These "seas," or maria, are actually areas which have few or no craters.

A LUNAR ROVING VEHICLE is an electric "car" the astronauts drove on the moon during the missions of *Apollo* 15, 16, and 17.

LUNOKHOD 1 (1970) USSR robot explorer ▶

12

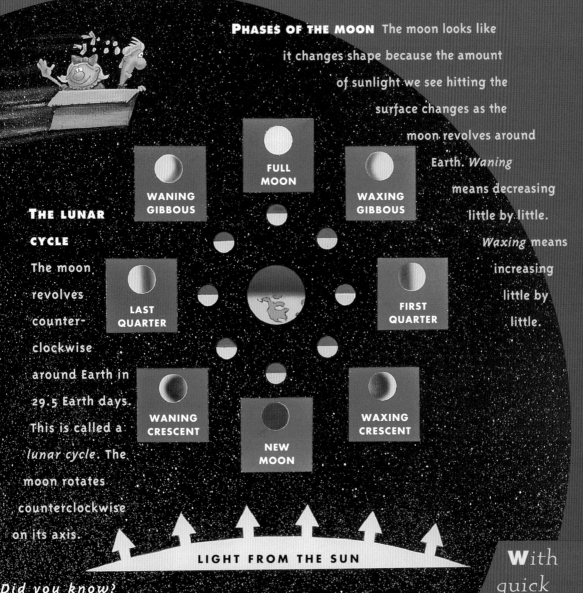

PHASES OF THE MOON The moon looks like it changes shape because the amount of sunlight we see hitting the surface changes as the moon revolves around Earth. *Waning* means decreasing little by little. *Waxing* means increasing little by little.

FULL MOON

WANING GIBBOUS

WAXING GIBBOUS

THE LUNAR CYCLE

The moon revolves counter-clockwise around Earth in 29.5 Earth days. This is called a *lunar cycle*. The moon rotates counterclockwise on its axis.

LAST QUARTER

FIRST QUARTER

WANING CRESCENT

NEW MOON

WAXING CRESCENT

LIGHT FROM THE SUN

Did you know?

Diameter (or width): 2,160 miles (about the same width as the United States)

Average distance from Earth: 239,000 miles

What would you weigh? If Connie and Bonnie weighed 100 pounds together on Earth, they'd weigh only 16 pounds on the moon.

What do you see?

With quick naviga-tion, they charted their course, then shot past the moon with incredible force. "Look over there — on that big rocky dune. Wave, Bonnie, wave! That's the Man in the Moon!"

13

The sun's diameter is 865,000 miles, or 109 times larger than the Earth's. One million Earths could fit inside the sun.

NOT ALL STARS ARE LIKE THE SUN

Stars come in many different colors, brightnesses, and sizes. Some are much bigger and some are much smaller than our sun.

THE SUN is just an ordinary star, but it just happens to be the center of our solar system. All the planets in our solar system revolve around the sun. The sun is a giant spinning ball of very hot gases (mostly hydrogen). Its temperature is over 10,000 degrees F. on the surface and nearly 10 million degrees F. in the center.

Then Bonnie complained, "It's getting quite hot. Perhaps we should navigate out of this spot." "Relax," replied Connie, "the fun's just begun! To get to the party, we must race 'round the sun."

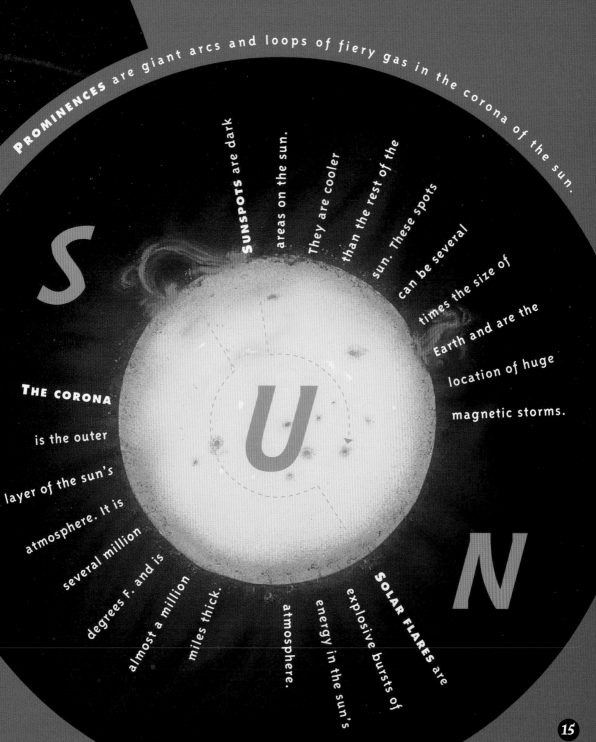

PROMINENCES are giant arcs and loops of fiery gas in the corona of the sun.

SUNSPOTS are dark areas on the sun. They are cooler than the rest of the sun. These spots can be several times the size of Earth and are the location of huge magnetic storms.

THE CORONA is the outer layer of the sun's atmosphere. It is several million degrees F. and is almost a million miles thick.

SOLAR FLARES are explosive bursts of energy in the sun's atmosphere.

S
U
N

MERCURY

MERCURY is the closest planet to the sun and is about half the size of Earth. It has no water, no atmosphere, no moons, and very little air. Its surface is much like the surface of our moon— dry, rocky, and covered with craters. Much of what we know about Mercury we learned from an American robot spacecraft named *Mariner 10*, which flew by Mercury in March 1974 and took pictures. Mercury is often known as the "metallic" planet because scientists think it has a large iron center.

Did you know?

Average distance from the sun: 36 million miles

Diameter: 3,031 miles

Number of moons: 0

Length of day: 1,408 Earth hours, or 58.65 Earth days

Length of year: 88 Earth days

What would you weigh? If Connie and Bonnie weighed 100 pounds together on Earth, they'd weigh 38 pounds on Mercury.

SUNBURN Since Mercury is so close to the sun and rotates slowly, each side of the planet has extreme temperatures. The side facing the sun may reach a scorching 750 degrees F. The side facing away from the sun can get down to -300 degrees F.

So on to the party with lightning-like speed! Connie glanced at the map and continued to read. "With the sun far behind us and the stars flying by, we'll soar over Mercury, barren and dry."

VENUS

is the second planet from the sun. It is covered by thick, yellow clouds made mostly of sulfuric acid. This thick atmosphere traps heat, making Venus the hottest planet in our solar system. Surface temperatures reach 900 degrees F. Even though Venus is hidden by clouds, scientists know there are many volcanoes erupting on its surface.

SLOW AND BACKWARDS

Venus has the slowest rotation of any of the planets, and it rotates backwards (clockwise). The spacecraft *Magellan* was launched May 4, 1989, by the shuttle *Atlantis*. It orbited Venus in August 1990, mapping the entire surface by radar.

Did you know?

Average distance from the sun: 67 million miles

Diameter: 7,521 miles

Number of moons: 0

Length of day: 5,832 Earth hours, or 243.02 Earth days

Length of year: 224.7 Earth days (the days on Venus are longer than the years!)

What would you weigh? If Connie and Bonnie weighed 100 pounds together on Earth, they'd weigh 90 pounds on Venus.

Venus

GODDESS OF LOVE AND BEAUTY

Following directions, they looked up above, "They named this one after the Goddess of Love. It's a planet called Venus," Connie read out aloud. "It's a very hot place in a thick yellow cloud."

Just then their small spacecraft was nudged off its trail by a very big comet and its million-mile tail. "Whew!" exclaimed Connie, downshifting a gear, "Comets are nice when they're not quite so near."

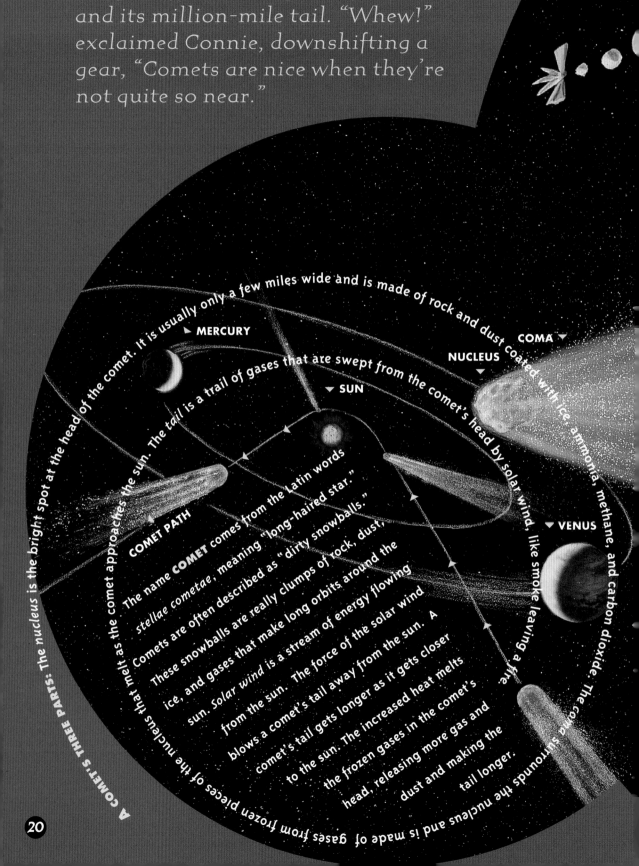

MERCURY

COMA

NUCLEUS

SUN

VENUS

COMET PATH

A COMET'S THREE PARTS: The nucleus is the bright spot at the head of the comet. It is usually only a few miles wide and is made of rock and dust coated with ice ammonia, methane, and carbon dioxide. The coma surrounds the nucleus and is made of gases from frozen pieces of the nucleus that melt as the comet approaches the sun. The *tail* is a trail of gases that are swept from the comet's head by solar wind, like smoke leaving a fire.

The name **COMET** comes from the Latin words *stellae cometae*, meaning "long-haired star." Comets are often described as "dirty snowballs." These snowballs are really clumps of rock, dust, ice, and gases that make long orbits around the sun. *Solar wind* is a stream of energy flowing from the sun. The force of the solar wind blows a comet's tail away from the sun. A comet's tail gets longer as it gets closer to the sun. The increased heat melts the frozen gases in the comet's head, releasing more gas and dust and making the tail longer.

TAIL

COMETS

THE HIGHS AND LOWS OF IT

Mars has volcanoes and canyons much bigger than any on Earth. Olympus Mons is a volcano wider than Arizona. Valles Marineos is a canyon five miles deeper than the Grand Canyon and as wide as America.

▼ OLYMPUS MONS

THE POLAR ICE CAPS on Mars are made of water, ice, and frozen carbon dioxide.

DUST STORMS on Mars can grow large enough

With the Earth at their backs, into space the twins sped. Then they spotted a planet all rocky and red. It was quite a relief — fuel was running real low. With a quick stop on Mars, they were ready to go.

MARS is the fourth planet from the sun. It is red, rocky, and about half the size of Earth. Its transparent atmosphere is made of poisonous carbon dioxide.

WHY IS MARS RED?

Its soil is covered with iron-rich minerals that combine with oxygen, forming a red dust called iron oxide.

THE MOONS OF MARS Mars has two tiny, potato-shaped moons, named Phobos and Deimos ("fear" and "panic") after two dogs of the god Mars. Phobos is 14 miles across and Deimos is nine miles across. Some astronomers think these two moons may be asteroids captured by Mars' gravity.

G O D   O F   W A R

to cover half the planet.

◄ PHOBOS

VALLES MARINEOS

PLUTO

EARTH

OUT THERE

DOWN

Did you know?

Average distance from the sun: 142 million miles

Diameter: 4,217 miles

Number of moons: 2

Length of day: 24.6 Earth hours

Length of year: 686.98 Earth days

What would you weigh? If Connie and Bonnie weighed 100

pounds together on Earth, they'd weigh 28 pounds on Mars.

A S T E

AN ASTEROID is a bumpy rock or minor planet orbiting the sun. There are over 3,450 asteroids that have known orbits and names, but there could be as many as 30,000. The largest asteroid, Ceres, is 620 miles in diameter. Others can be as small as pebbles.

The journey was smooth; not a bump could be felt until they flew into the asteroid belt. Half a million small planets made flying a trick, but the twins sailed right through them with hardly a nick.

24

WHERE DO ASTEROIDS COME FROM?

Experts once believed that they were remains of former planets. It is now believed that they are fragments left from the beginnings of the solar system.

The five largest asteroids

——————— Diameter in miles

CERES............................620

PALLAS.......................375

VESTA......................332

HYGEIA..............278

EUPHROSYNE...228

R O I D S

orbiting between Mars and Jupiter

Did you know?

Average distance from the sun: 483 million miles

Diameter: 88,703 miles

Number of moons: 16

Length of day: 9.8 Earth hours

Length of year: 12 Earth years, or 4,380 Earth days

What would you weigh? If Connie and Bonnie weighed 100 pounds together on Earth, they'd weigh 287 pounds on Jupiter.

The "Great Red Spot" on Jupiter is a storm of whirling clouds made of gases. This spot is twice as big as Earth and over 300 years old.

THE MOONS OF JUPITER Twelve of Jupiter's moons are very small, but four of

They saw on the map that they'd soon have to pass four very large planets made of liquid and gas. The first one was Jupiter — the largest of all. It makes all the others look puny and small.

J U P I T E R

KING OF THE GODS

JUPITER, the fifth planet from the sun, is the largest planet in our solar system. It is a gigantic ball of hydrogen and helium with many fierce storms on its surface. People on Earth are hoping to learn much more about Jupiter. On October 18, 1989, the satellite *Galileo* — named after the famous discoverer of Jupiter's four largest moons — was launched to reach Jupiter in December of 1995 and to take detailed photos of the giant planet.

Jupiter has sixteen moons, and four of them are the size of planets. The largest moon, Ganymede, is larger than the planet Mercury.

SATURN is the second-largest planet in our solar system and the sixth planet from the sun. It is made of such gases as ammonia, hydrogen, methane, and helium. Because Saturn's gravity is so strong, these gases are squeezed tightly together and turned into liquids. Saturn has at least 18 moons. Its largest moon is called Titan.

GOD OF AGRICULTURE

SATURN

Did you know?

Average distance from the sun: 886 million miles

Diameter: 74,600 miles

Number of moons: 18 known

Length of day: 10.53 Earth hours

Length of year: 29.5 Earth years, or 10,767.5 Earth days

What would you weigh? If Connie and Bonnie weighed 100 pounds together on Earth, they'd weigh 132 pounds on Saturn.

Then hanging a left, they saw — of all things — a strange-looking planet surrounded by rings. These rings around Saturn are pieces of ice. It's too cold to land on, but the view sure is nice.

BATH TIME Saturn is so light that if you could find a bathtub big enough to hold it, it would float.

SATURN'S RINGS are made of millions of pieces of rock, dust, and ice — from tiny chunks to pieces up to seven miles across. The rings are less than one mile thick but stretch 238,000 miles across — the distance between the earth and the moon!

URANUS is known as the "tilted" planet because it looks like it's spinning on its side. It is the seventh planet from the sun, blue-green in color, and is only half the size of Jupiter and Saturn. Little was known about Uranus and Neptune until *Voyager 2* flew past them and took photographs in 1986.

An odd blue-
green planet
was
approaching
quite fast.
It spun on its side
as they went
zooming past.
"There goes
Uranus!" Connie
said with a
cheer. "This means
that the party is
getting quite near."

BACKWARDS
PLANET
Uranus is one of
the three planets
that rotate
"backwards"
(clockwise). Do
you remember the
other two?

U R A N U S

GOD OF THE HEAVENS
URANUS

HEY! TURN ON THE LIGHTS! Half of Uranus is in sunlight for 42 Earth years, then in darkness for another 42 Earth years.

Did you know?

Average distance from the sun: 1,865 million miles

Diameter: 31,800 miles

Number of moons: 15

Length of day: 17.23 Earth hours

Length of year: 84 Earth years

What would you weigh? If Connie and Bonnie weighed 100 pounds together on Earth, they'd weigh 93 pounds on Uranus.

RING...RING...Uranus has eleven rings, which are hard to see.

•• T R I T O N ••

that orbits in the opposite direction of the spin of its planet.

Did you know?

Average distance from the sun: 2,793 million miles

Diameter: 30,770 miles

Number of moons: 8

Length of day: 16.04 Earth hours

Length of year: 165 Earth years, or 60,225 Earth days

What would you weigh? If Connie and Bonnie weighed 100 pounds together on Earth, they'd weigh 123 pounds on Neptune.

"**N**ow
there's a
great sight,
Bonnie —
don't you agree?
It's the planet named
after the god of the sea."
"You can tell that it is Neptune
by its giant dark spot — a storm
that looks like an Earth-sized
ink blot."

is the eighth planet from the sun. It is a very stormy planet with strong winds. Both Neptune

N E P T U N E

WAY OUT THERE Sometimes Neptune is the farthest planet from the sun! Pluto's orbit around the sun is a different shape from Neptune's, and so sometimes Pluto is nearer the sun than Neptune. (See the diagram of their orbital paths on page 5.) Neptune has been the farthest planet from the sun since 1979 and will be until 1999. In 1999, Pluto's elliptical orbit will take it out past Neptune again.

Do you remember what an elliptical orbit looks like?

◄ GREAT DARK SPOT

N E P T U N E

God of the sea

The twins took a peek at a bright galaxy — billions of stars were all they could see. The two were quite hungry after traveling all day, so they grabbed a big bite of the great Milky Way.

▼ ORION NEBULAE

A LIGHT-YEAR is the distance light travels in one year. Light travels almost six trillion miles in one year, so one light-year is almost six trillion miles. Many stars are hundreds of light-years away!

WARNING: Galaxies may appear closer than they really are. Some galaxies are billions of light-years away. From Earth, it would be impossible to get the view of the different galaxies that Connie and Bonnie are now enjoying. **ANDROMEDA GALAXY** The closest galaxy to Earth is this spiral galaxy two million light-years from Earth. It can barely be seen with the naked eye.

WHAT ARE NEBULAE?

Giant clouds of gas and dust between stars where new stars may be forming.

▲ M13

What are Nebulae? Giant clouds of gas and dust between stars where new stars may be forming

CRAB NEBULAE ▷

SEVEN SISTERS

THE MILKY WAY

WHIRLPOOL GALAXY ▷

GALAXIES
AND NEBULAE

◀ RING NEBULAE

GALAXIES are the largest forms in the universe. They are huge collections of stars, dust, and gas. There can be a few million to hundreds of billions of stars in a galaxy. **GALAXIES** come in many shapes and sizes. A galaxy may appear as a spiral shape (like our own Milky Way), an oval (or elliptical) shape, or an irregular shape.

SOMBRERO GALAXY ▶

NOT JUST A CANDY BAR!

Earth is part of a galaxy called the **MILKY WAY**, which has about 10 billion stars. Its bright stars form four spiraling arms with a ring-shaped group of stars called the "nucleus" in the center. Beyond the Milky Way there are billions of other galaxies.

Bonnie grew restless. "We've traveled quite far —I think that I've seen every moon, every star! I'm ready to party and munch on some cake, unbend my legs and give them a shake."

A STAR is a body of gas that makes intense heat and light through "nuclear fusion" — a process that turns hydrogen into helium and releases incredible amounts of energy. This energy makes stars appear to shine.

HOW A STAR DIES A star doesn't shine forever. The hydrogen at the center of a star eventually burns low. Then the star swells up to 100 times its original size. These huge stars turn red and are called "red giants." When a star's fuel burns out, it explodes.

HOW MANY STARS ARE THERE? There are billions and billions of stars in our galaxy. Only 6,000 can be seen from Earth.

OUR STAR THE SUN The sun, the closest star to Earth, is 93 million miles away. The next nearest star, Alpha Centauri, is four light-years away. Do you remember how long one light-year is?

RED ◄ cool WHITE hot ► BLUE

Stars can be many different colors. These colors depend on the age and temperature of the star.

WHAT IS A CONSTELLATION? A group of stars that can be seen from Earth. There are 88 constellations. Most are named after characters in ancient Greek myths because early astronomers imagined that the outlines of these constellations looked like certain mythological figures. The location of the constellations in the sky guided travelers and sailors as they journeyed.

GEMINI ▶

STARS

ORION ▶

◀ CANIS MAJOR

CLOSE, AND YET SO FAR...
Even though stars in the same constellation look close together, they may be very far from each other. The stars Alpha Centauri and Beta Centauri seem very close together but are actually 440 light-years apart.

Pluto's moon is only 11,640 miles from the planet.
Our moon is over 239,000 miles from Earth.

CHARON

PLUTO

GOD OF THE UNDERWORLD

THAT'S COLD!

The surface of Pluto
is covered with a
layer of methane ice.
The temperature is
about -369 degrees F.

PLUTO *is a dark, mysterious planet. The
sun looks 900 times fainter on this planet than
it does on Earth. Pluto was discovered in 1930
because it was pulling Neptune off its expected
orbit. Pluto and its moon, Charon, are almost the
same size, and Pluto is smaller than Earth's
moon. Charon, Pluto's moon, is only 11,640
miles away from the planet. In
contrast, our moon is over
239,000 miles from Earth.*

YES, BACKWARDS

Pluto is one of the three planets
that rotates clockwise.

38

FAR-OUT! Most people think Pluto is the farthest planet from the sun, but this isn't always true. During part of its year, Pluto's orbit goes inside the orbit of Neptune. Sometimes Neptune is the farthest planet from the sun.

Then Connie yelled out, "That's Pluto I see!" "We've made it! We've made it!" the twins cried with glee. A balloon led them down to a creature below. They gave it their gift, then were in for a show.

It ripped from
the present the ribbon
of red, then picked up the gift, and bit off its head.
"I've never tried these — it seems such a waste! It's by
far the best present I ever did taste."

E a r

THE ATMOSPHERE is a layer of air 220 miles thick that surrounds the Earth.

And then the twins noticed it was getting quite late — they'd said they'd be home by a quarter till eight. They waved their farewells amidst laughter and mirth, then retraced their path back to home, Mother Earth.

It protects life on Earth from extreme temperatures and the sun's harmful radiation.

"MOTHER EARTH" is the third planet from the sun and the largest of the inner planets. Earth is the only planet in our solar system that can support life-forms.

Did you know?

Average distance from the sun: 94.24 million miles	Length of day: 24 hours
Diameter: 7,926 miles	Length of year: 365.24 days
Number of moons: 1	What do you weigh on Earth?

EARTH'S THREE MAJOR PARTS

1. The **CORE** is the middle of the planet, consisting of extremely hot metallic material.

2. The **MANTLE** is a liquid rock layer surrounding the core.

3. The **CRUST** is the hardened top layer covering the mantle. Earth's crust is between five and 25 miles thick.

Bonnie was frantic. "We're landing too fast! The last thing I want is a full-body cast!" The craft spun 'round once with a quick somersault, then rolled up some turf and ground to a halt.

Bonnie was pale and let out a sigh, gave Connie a poke and stared at the sky. "No more adventure! Let's stay in the yard! For next year's grand party, we'll just send a card!"

Illustration by Barry Bruce

ABOUT THE AUTHORS

Ray Nelson Jr. started looking at stars the day he learned to walk. Unfortunately, they're not the kind of stars you'll learn about in this book. They're not even the kind of stars you'll find in Hollywood. They're the kind of stars you get when you bump your head a lot. (Ray's a rather clumsy individual.) While growing up, Ray loved to draw goofy pictures and write silly stories. It seemed only natural that he should write and illustrate books for kids. Ray currently lives in Portland, Oregon, with his wife, Theresa, his daughter, Alexandria, and a mutant dog named Molly. (Molly weighs three thousand pounds, has a brain the size of a peanut, and drools a ton . . . even for a Great Dane.)

Douglas Kelly is a very talented artist. Ray tricked him into leaving a real job with a regular paycheck so they could work together making books. Doug credits a great deal of his artistic talent to his father, who was an artist and a printer. (Doug's co-workers credit the ink fumes in his dad's print shop for Doug's weird personality.) He trained formally to become an artist at Art Center College of Design. Doug currently lives in a toolshed in the back of Ray's yard — located right next to Molly's dog run. His best friends are Victoria and Toonces the cat.

Kari Rasmussen and Julie Mohr are two incredibly talented and hard-working individuals. They spent the last six months working as interns helping put together *Connie & Bonnie's Birthday Blastoff*. (They will probably need the next six months for therapy.)

SPECIAL THANKS

We would like to thank the following individuals for their help in producing *Connie & Bonnie's Birthday Blastoff*: Jim Todd and David Heil of OMSI, Mike and Holly McLane, Jeff and Kathryn Nuss, George Evans, Theresa and Alexandria Nelson, Victoria Collins, Chris Nelson, Connie Kelly, Ted Owen and Kathleen Barnebey, Barry Bruce, Edna Nelson, Irv and Louise Nuss, Trisha Mohr, Janet Lockwood, Mike and Jennifer Jacobson, Kelly Kuntz, Spock, Mark and Jennifer Hansen, Tracy and Stewart Sandor, Sig and Tricia Paulsen, Gary and Marilyn Schoos, Deborah and Joel Beilman, and Michelle Fritzler.